MY SILENT STORY

Ooooh, I'm Telling...

Overcoming The Brokenness of Sexual Abuse

GISELE VANN

Table of Contents

Dedication

I would like to dedicate this book to my husband, Vernon; and my children and grandchildren.

You are so special to me because you have loved me unconditionally throughout this journey.

To my awesome husband Vernon, thank you so much for your support, love, and patience. To my Mom and Daddy, Vera and Anthony Emanuel, thank you. To my amazing children, it's an honor to be your mother. I thank God for each and every one of you. To my wonderful grandchildren, Nana loves you all.

Acknowledgements

Special people I would like to thank for helping me on my life's journey and helping me write this book are Vera Emanuel (my mom), Dana Hicks, Valerie Sharp, Jessica Johns, Joshua Hicks, Jordan Hicks, Jeffery Hicks, Matthew Hicks, Emanuel Hicks, Prophetess Beverly Anike, Portia Pennington and Irene Case.

I know I can't acknowledge everyone that has poured into my life, but I want to give a special Thank You to my mother, Vera Emanuel, for her support along the way.

Thank you to my daughter-in-law, Dana Hicks, for all your help.

Thank you to my sisters, Valerie Emanuel and Jessica Johns, for your unconditional love and support.

Thank you to my sons, Joshua Hicks, Jordan Hicks, Jeffrey Hicks, Matthew Hicks and Emanuel Hicks, for cheering me on along the way.

I also want to thank my kingdom sister, Prophetess Beverly Anike, for her words of wisdom and encouragement.

Thank you to my sweet dear friend, Wanita Branch, for words of wisdom and always giving me clear and honest counsel.

Thank you to my niece, Portia Pennington. Your support has never failed to surprise me. And to Irene Case, for all of her help through the years.

Just know you all hold a special place in my heart; I truly love you all.

I am grateful for this journey, and I thank God for His love for me.

Foreword

It is with pleasure and delight to be given the honor of painting a portrait of my amazing, authentic and priceless masterpiece of sister Gisele (GG). When I say authentic, it describes the scene when she was born. I thought God had made a mistake by placing her in the family, but at her birth, I knew God had gotten it right. Her compassionate and passionate story will ignite the desire for a deeper revelation of who we truly are: An authentic, one-of-a-kind masterpiece created by God, always evolving. I love you, Gisele.

Valerie Emanuel

Introduction

"Oooh... I'm Telling"

My life changed forever that Saturday morning. The carefree life I had was no more. It is so important for me to remember when the sexual abuse began because that's when I started to feel empty inside. Something shifted inside of me. I did not look at the world the same way anymore. I didn't want to be around people. There was sadness in my eyes, and I was no longer happy.

While laying on my back with that person on top of me, I was thinking to myself: "How did I get here? Why me?" My whole body was in pain. It felt like a pile of bricks stacked on my entire body from my head to my feet! I was nine years old at the time. I weighed about 60 pounds. But it was not a stack of bricks on me, it was a male family member, pounding into me like a jackhammer! I wanted to yell or scream out to release the pain I was experiencing. It was overwhelming, but nothing came out of my mouth, not even a sound. It got to a point, I remember, that I would just lay there like a log. I would literally go numb. I <u>never</u> got used to it, but I got tired of fighting, so I would just lay there and let it happen and pretend that I was somewhere else until he finished. It seemed like the time he was on top of me got longer and longer. I HATED EVERY MINUTE HE WAS ON ME! I hated the act and the person doing the act! I <u>did not</u> enjoy anything about the abuse! That question has come up too many times, so let me tell you how it felt: It hurt. It was very painful! I was nine years old! My virginity was taken from me, and the pain did not let up during the three years the abuse went on! So now you know my truth.

I have been asked the questions: "Why didn't you tell your parents?" or "Why did you just lay there?" or "Why did you let the abuse happen? Did you enjoy it?" WOW! The answer to all those questions is first, it was them that kept doing this to me! Someone even said to me, "You didn't stop them." I was scared and confused. I felt I had no control over my own body. And hell no I wasn't enjoying it! I was ashamed of myself. I felt dirty, unloved, unwanted, used and exploited because some selfish individuals misused their authority and took my virginity from me! YES, I was confused, angry and enraged; it became worse the older I got. I hated those individuals at one time in my life. Being abused opened so many negative doors in my life that I could not close until I dealt with everything that came with the abuse. I had to make a change. I did not like who I had become. I knew this was not what it was supposed to be.

I remember that I absolutely loved Saturday mornings growing up. It was just a good time to recover from the busy week and have breakfast together as a family. It was a joyous time for me. We had a big family. There were nine of us. My dad would work all week long. On Saturday, I would hear my parents talking in their room and I would lay in my bed until the talking would stop or I heard their footsteps in the kitchen. That would be my signal to get up. Most of the time, my dad did the cooking. I loved when he cooked because he would cook just about anything in the kitchen. I loved the variety with so many different scents; the aroma was amazing! We all sat down at the kitchen table and talked about the events of the week. That was a joyful time in my childhood.

Then I remember the not so happy times on Saturdays, when I would endure the horrifying events that took place. They occurred for three years with the same pain, but a different person, three in all. Each time they climbed on top of me, something was taken away from me. Not just my virginity, but each time someone climbed on top of me, something was taken internally, like my self-worth. It broke my spirit and my heart. It stripped me of my emotions. It was like robbers pushing their way into my house and taking everything out and leaving me with nothing but empty walls (my soul). I felt bare inside and out. I felt all alone and unloved. Now I was this empty soul in the world just breathing without a purpose, plan, or drive. I started filling those empty places with hopelessness.

At the same time, I started holding on to unforgiveness and hate deep in my heart. I built up so much animosity toward so many people during those three years of abuse. It seemed like my heart was full of negativity. There was no room for anything else. I was angry at myself. I hated myself for someone else's actions. Crazy, but true. I did not like myself at all. Life looked grim in my eyes. I was surrounded by a big family. All of my needs and wants were taken care of, but yet, I felt invisible most of my childhood. My oldest sister told me that I was extremely shy and unsure of myself. I remember feeling dirty, ugly, and dumb, like an outcast. I excelled in sports, which built up some confidence, but the problem was I was not dealing with the root of the problem.

Life happened. Elementary school, middle school, high school, college, and marriage at the age of nineteen.

I became a stepmom to four children at nineteen. I had an abortion, and a miscarriage, and gave birth to my four sons. Then my husband of 19 ½ years was diagnosed with cancer, and I became a widow and a single mother of four at age 36. There was sadness in my heart from his passing. I wanted to take my own life after the death of my husband, not because of his passing, but because the pressure of being a single mom was overwhelming. All through these events in my life, my heart was still full of the negativity I stored from when I was nine years old and did not allow anything to take the place of all of those negative thoughts.

Different events happened in my life that made me happy, but they were just temporary and the negative mindset was still right there waiting to get its place back in my head. The sexual abuse had broken my spirit into pieces, and my emotions were all over the place. I was walking through life, and everything in the physical was intact with my outside appearance looking like I was training for a marathon while my inside felt like it was taking its last breath. Somewhere in the back of my mind, I knew something good would come out of the madness that happened in my childhood. The good and bad that happened made me who I am today. I had days and nights full of flashbacks of abuse. Back then, I thought that if I could just forget about the childhood abuse and keep busy and move away from where it happened and the people who did it and start my own family, it would eventually be erased from my mind. But I found out that it doesn't work like that.

I don't remember the exact day or month that I realized I was worth the work and the time and the effort to address my childhood abuse. I was moving through life with this leech that was sucking the life out of me day by day for years. I was so tired mentally and physically, and fed up in the way my life was going, and I surely did not want to hand down this hurt and despair to my children and grandchildren. The negative effects of abuse had my life static and torpid for years. I had to make up my mind to turn my life around. There was so much that opposed me, but a great door of opportunity for successful favor has been unlocked for me. Not of my own choosing, but there's nothing in all of heaven and earth that can stop God's will and His work that He will do in me and through me.

"...because a wide door for effective service has opened to me [in Ephesus, a very promising opportunity], and there are many adversaries." Corinthians 16:9)

That let me know God was always in control. Even when I was abused, He was in control; He chose that event to be a part of my journey.

"And we know [with great confidence] that God [who is deeply concerned about us] causes all things to work together [as a plan] for good for those who love God, to those who are called according to His plan and purpose." Romans 8:28)

God had a purpose for me the whole time. He allowed the abuse to be a part of my journey. He knew I was going to come out on top either way! I overcame the abuse to help someone else get through. I'm writing this to show that you can overcome the feeling of terror, fear, shame, guilt and rage. I know. I had all of these feelings and then some. Depression, self blame, low self-esteem, and delays in learning, but I overcame them all and you can, too. So let's do this!

My mind was made up to do whatever it took to break free of bondage. I had to take the first step myself; no one can do it for you. I tried to go the route of having someone else do the work for me, and it didn't work out in my favor. It hindered me in the long run. I had a lot of setbacks, but I was determined to break through and be set free. As I walked through my journey of healing, I found my purpose. Knowing my purpose is where I discovered my worth, and knowing my worth opened so many other areas in my life that had laid dormant for a long time.

Ooooh I'm Telling .... Because it's easy to try to cover up the abuse in your life, but the fact is, it's not going to go away until you deal with it. I chose to live in ways that are pleasing to God, and he continues to make even my enemies be at peace with me.

"When a man's ways please the Lord, He makes even his enemies to be at peace with him." Proverbs 16:7)

I had to change my focus. I stopped focusing on what happened to me (the abuse) and put my focus and trust in who made me and found out what His word said about my situation.

When you make up your mind that you are tired of carrying the weight that goes along with sexual abuse — or any abuse — things will change. As you read this book you are going to be a witness, along with those around you, of your own transformation into the person you were born to be.

ARE YOU READY TO LIGHTEN YOUR LOAD? I believe and hope this book takes you to your next level in life. Love yourself and embrace your past to catch a ride into your future and use your ticket to fly high into your present.

"Do not put your trust in the ways of man, nor do I rely on the strength of others to sustain me. My trust is in the Lord — my provider. He alone is the strength of my life." Based on Jeremiah 17:5 & 7)

Chapter 1

Saturday Morning

"Oooh... I'm Telling"

I will never forget sitting in Sunday school shaking and scared out of my wits. Praying so hard that the Sunday school teacher, Deacon Isom, would <u>NOT</u> call me to be the next person to read out loud to the class from the Sunday school book. Yes! That would be me. I am the seventh child of nine children.

I grew up in Southern California in a middle-class family. My dad worked hard for the life we lived. There were nine of us children. I had five brothers and three sisters, and we never went without. In my eyes, I was born into the perfect family, but as time went by, I realized that "perfect" was not the word for my family. The phrase that best described my family was a "work in progress." I believe my parents did the best job they knew how in raising us.

But things changed for me in the worst way. At nine years old, I was raped by three of my family members. Not only was my virginity taken on that hot day in the desert, something shifted inside of me that day. In this book, I will walk you through my preparation for the earthquake of emotions and the tsunami of anger that consumed me. It was a flood of emotions that nearly drowned me for years to come.

This book is about how I not only overcame sexual abuse as a child, but through it all, how I did not give up on myself and didn't want these actions to repeat in the next generation. These are the two reasons that gave me the push and desire to get healed. I needed to do everything possible to get help and overcome the deep hurt and unforgiveness that had consumed my emotions far too long. Ooooh! I'm Telling ... Is my story of the struggles, setbacks, and rejections I had to endure, as well as the triumphs over the dark tunnels I had to walk through.

I'm writing this book to share a message of hope with anyone who has ever been abused. There is a way out for you. I want to share with you how I worked my way through a whirlwind of mixed emotions and the feelings of shame, guilt, and learning disabilities while recovering from a traumatic experience. It is so important for you to know that you can live a life of forgiveness and freedom from the abuse you encounter. There is a life of peace and love in the gratifying life you deserve. There is a rewarding and dynamic future waiting for you in spite of your having been abused.

The first thing you need to know is that you are valuable, precious, and priceless! You are worth the effort of the process of being healed, and you can become a conqueror and a champion to overcome abuse. It does not define you or the direction of your life! It was a part of your life, not your whole life. Keep in mind as you read this book that this is not only for you but for the next generation, too. You don't want your grandchildren to go through the same hell you went through when you confront all that comes with being abused. The first step is making up your mind that you are not going to let the person or persons who abused you control you by holding on to the unforgiveness and shame that came with being violated. The time is now for you to walk into what God has for you. Shake off the pain of the past and dive fearlessly into your future!

I wrote this book for anyone who has been abused in any way as a child or as an adult, male or female. It is for those who struggle with the effects of the abuse such as low self-esteem, social isolation, flashbacks, learning disabilities, or the feelings of shame and guilt so much that your life is stagnant. Ultimately when you walk away after reading this book, you could be free from the effects or on your way to a life of freedom. You will learn how to love and value yourself and not blame yourself for someone else's actions that violated you and learn the tools needed to live your life in forgiveness and freedom!

My hope after you read this book is that you have the resources needed:

- To activate the person you are truly meant to be.
- To uncover your purpose in life.
- To be free of the negative mindset, hurt and anger that was holding you back.
- To have the courage to remove the masks and the mindset of lies from your thoughts.
- To expose the imposter and remove all the negative effects of the abuse.

If you have an infection in your heart, it will affect your entire body! Let's get your heart healthy first, and it will affect your whole life. Heal yourself first and everything else will line up!

"When you pass through the waters I will be with you; and through the rivers, they will not overwhelm you. When you walk through fire, you will not be scorched, Nor will the flame burn you." Isaiah 43:2

Just remember: God is with you all the time. He is all knowing! Even when I was being abused, God was there. It was hard for me to believe that at first, but I know He was there. When you go through the fire, God is there; and when you come out of the fire, you will not be burned — you won't even smell like smoke!

I was sexually abused ... but God ... He brought me out of the pain and hurt and the unforgiveness. I have overcome, and I am living a life of freedom!

After reading this book, you will be able to experience the same life God has given me despite the abuse. My deep and committed respect for my heavenly father places my wisdom on open display for all to see. When I humble myself in His presence, of His majesty, He lifts me to the place of highest honor.

"Wisdom's instruction is to fear the Lord and humility comes before honor." Proverbs 15:33

It doesn't matter what's in your past. God has a way of escape for you, and it's going to work for your good. Just know that the victory belongs to you! Run the victory laps called life!

Chapter 2

Discovering Your Voice

"Oooh... I'm Telling"

This is about finding your voice and using it! Letting your voice be heard and having the courage to speak up and not be silent anymore. Standing up for yourself, knowing when and how to speak into your life and your destiny. Knowing that you have a voice in what happens in your future. It's not about the people or the person who abused you! That's the progression I finally made in my life where I had to speak up for myself and walk in confidence; that it was OK for me to take care of myself and not wait for someone else to do it. Once you find that voice and activate it for your advantage, that's when change comes!

I didn't know I had a voice until later in life. The way I discovered that I had a voice was from within ... It was buried under deep hurt. I thought for a long time that my voice was taken away from me when the abuse started, but it was there all the time, it was just masked by shame and hurt. It's like when you're sitting on the patio and an annoying fly keeps landing on you, you shoo him away, only to discover that you have a fly swatter an arm's length away. All you must do is take control of the situation. You have the ability to change anything! Just go ahead and kill the annoying fly and move on. You can do the same thing about the negative thoughts you have about yourself. YOU have the power to take control over who speaks the loudest in your head. Control starts when you allow it. Stop allowing those negative thoughts to be the loudest "voices" (or thoughts) in your head. It all starts with you. You can't change the past, but you can take charge of your present and your future. Your thoughts make you good or bad. You have to start controlling what you allow to "speak" loudest in your head. You are the only one who can do that. Start by taking one day at a time and start speaking life into yourself.

When you first start, you may feel silly; at least I did. I can't tell you how long it's going to take before you start believing it, but the key is don't stop. There are going to be some days when you want to stop, but you must encourage yourself. Don't wait for someone else to do what you can do for yourself. You must know that you have a grand purpose in this world as you take charge of your thoughts about yourself and gear them toward the positive and pure. Slowly but surely, those loud "voices" (negative thoughts) that had free reign in your head for years are pushed out as you replace them with thoughts that are uplifting to you and your new outlook on life. These should be thoughts that are cheerleaders for you and are encouraging you to be a better you. It's not going to happen overnight, and let me tell you this, those negative thoughts with loud "voices" that have been in your head for years and dominating your thoughts will not leave without a fight: They are relentless. But you will win if you are resilient, just like I did. You must keep going and not give in.

You have to look yourself in the mirror and tell yourself that you are determined to change your thoughts, and it will change your vocabulary. Changing your vocabulary will change your actions, and changing your actions will change your life! What you choose to allow to go on in your head is up to you. To take charge makes a big difference in your life. The thoughts in your head determine which in direction your life will head. Words influence your heart, and your actions draw a picture of your everyday life. The first person you have to make peace with is yourself. I was ready for a change in my life, and I had to start by changing my mindset. It wasn't the easiest thing to do but in the end, it did get easier. I was determined to turn my thinking to a positive place. Whatever YOU think about YOU matters, and once you understand that and approach things differently, others will follow your lead. First, make up your mind about who you are and whose you are for yourself. It may take some time for you to have confidence in yourself, but if you keep feeding yourself positive and uplifting words, eventually you're going to start believing those words and the voice of truth will be louder than the lies of those negative words.

"God has laid before you, in His word, the way of life and the way of death. It is up to you to choose which way to live." Based on Jeremiah 21:8

I choose life.

It is so important to stand firm. It all starts with you wanting to make a change in your life. You are the only one that controls what kind of mindset you have. Don't allow other people in your life to tell you who you are or what you are. It's not up to them; you give them that power when you accept what they say about you. It is a double whammy when it comes from your family members and your friends.

They know you the best, and they know what buttons to push and love pushing them. You have to take matters into your own hands. I was not going to allow sexual abuse to dictate the precious time I had left on this earth. It was time for me to start loving myself just the way God made me, not hold my head down because something unpleasant happened to me. I had my life ahead of me, and I was tired of waking up every morning to a pity party! The sad thing is that the same people show up to the party. People saying: you are ugly, you are not smart, no one will ever love you, you are damaged goods. Those were just some of the people who would show up to my pity party. I made up my mind that I needed to stop letting just anybody come to the parties in my head. I had to make a guest list and give out invitations and have a guard stationed and only let in those who had an invitation.

I had to take charge of what I allowed to set in my mind. The negative image I had of myself was weighing me down in so many ways in my life, and I was tired of the load. The weight of the past was making me walk slower, and in some areas in my life, I was stagnant. But the good thing was, I was not comfortable where my life was going and where the negativity was leading me. The fight was in my head, and I had a mindset that was not leading me down the right path. I was happy when I changed paths by changing my mindset. The way I did that was to start speaking words of life, words that made me want to get out of bed, and not only get up, but encourage others around me! To push hard and fight for my peace of mind. Even after I totally surrendered to the "Prince of Peace," the right mindset didn't come easy. First, I had to make a choice. That's when the battle started. I was not going to stand by anymore and let self-doubt rule my mind. I knew I had to do something. So, I did. I made the choice to make a change for the good.

It is so important to know first that you have a voice that needs to be heard. That your opinion about what you think about yourself matters. That it is OK to speak up and stand up for yourself. To encourage, uplift and push yourself and love yourself. It's important to tell yourself that you are worth it. That you will reach your dreams and not just have a good life but an *amazing* life. That you have a built-in cheering section that is loud and positive. It all starts with you taking that first step within yourself.

The first thing you need to do is to love yourself. To know that "voice" within. If the "voice" you hear is not for you, don't accept the lies if it doesn't line up with the person you were created to be. You can learn how to manage your "voice" (thoughts), and the way you do that is to reject every negative word that comes up in your mind. It's like if we are training for a bodybuilding competition. You first start training your muscles to get used to the weight, you keep training and eventually your muscles get tired and sore. Some days you think to yourself, "I'm so uncomfortable, my muscles hurt, I'm just going to stop training even before I see my results." That's the same way it goes with changing your mindset. It will get uncomfortable. There will be days when you want to go back to the old way of thinking because there was no resistance, no fight. The old way of thinking allowed the negative words to have dominion over my mind because they had no competition. But when I made the change, that's when the fight began. I kept on pushing down those negative words. You must speak up and let the words that are encouraging be the loudest "voice" you hear. Yes, you can do this. It doesn't matter how long you've had this negative mindset; you can turn it around if you really want to. If you change your mindset, you can change your life. Not only your life, but your children's lives and even the next generation! This is not just for you, you're making this change for many other people. Changing your mindset eventually becomes changing your actions. Everything starts in your mind. Control your thoughts and you will have control of your life.

I remember when the plane landed in Italy. I was exhausted. It was a thirteen-hour flight to meet my husband there. I was starting a new life in a new country far away from everyone I ever knew. I was among strangers and only I knew about my past. I felt free, but then I figured out it's not about anyone else or what country I was in. It was about my mindset and choosing what "voice" I was going to allow to dominate my thoughts. I thought that if I moved to a new country away from everyone who knew me and started fresh, my past would just vanish and those negative thoughts would stop. I was so excited and scared at the same time. I didn't know the language or the culture, but I was there to learn. That's when something within me shifted. What I mean by that is that my mindset changed, and I started looking at myself in a new light. It wasn't about where I lived or who knew about my past. It was about me. It all started with wanting to make a change in my thoughts.

Did I want to continue to allow those negative thoughts to have the loudest "voice" in my head, or did I want to change my thought pattern about myself? It was difficult at first. My mind was used to the negative mindset. It was easy for my mind to take the path it was used to. I started speaking words of life to myself, but at the same time, those thoughts of self-doubt rose up to override my new way of thinking. It was a fight in my head, and it was up to me to decide who was going to win! I was in it to win it! I had made a promise to myself that the negative thoughts had to change. The only person who could do that was me. I had to move to a new country for my eyes to be opened to this truth. That's when I realized that I had control over my mindset, me and only me. I had to start training my mind to think positive and to drive out words that were defeating me. It felt like an uphill battle, but I pushed through the pain. I woke up every morning thanking God for one more day. It's very important to start your day with positive words before you get out of bed. All through the day I would speak phases to myself like:

"I can do this."
"I'm who I want to be."
"I'm strong."
 "I'm enough."

I didn't believe what I was saying at first, but I didn't stop. I kept encouraging myself day after day. It did not matter what was going on in my life at the time, I would find something good from it. I start looking at me and my life with a new set of eyes because I changed my mindset.

What you think about yourself is what you will be. Yes, it will be a struggle when you first start out. The reason for that is your mind was used to one path for years and you have to start training it to go down a new and improved path that has never been used before. It's going to take time for you to break in that path by being consistent in managing your thoughts and rejecting all the negative words that enter your mind. But you are worth it! No one else is going to know your worth until *you* know your worth! The more

I started telling myself how amazing I was, guess what? I started believing it, and I started acting like I was amazing and walking like I was amazing. When I convinced myself by speaking words of truth over my life, things changed for me in a big way! I started walking differently. My eyes had been closed for so long. How you view yourself is so important because it is how other people will see you.

Don't wait: You can take the first step if you want to change your mindset. Start right now speaking life to yourself; don't wait for anyone else to do it. You have your whole life ahead of you, don't let the pain of your past dictate your future. Use the pain of the past to propel you not only in your present but also in your future as well. It's all in your hands. Do not allow someone else's mistakes to dominate your life. You hold the position to control what "voice" speaks the loudest in your head. It's your choice. You can speak negative words that tear you down, have you doubting yourself and hating yourself on so many levels, or you can choose positive words that will help push you to the next level in life. Words that uplift you and encourage you. Cutting all ties from the past, not just sitting by and letting negative words run rampant in your head. You will be able to make the right decisions so you can live your life to the fullest.

You can change your mindset! When you change your mindset, you change your life. You know you need to change your mindset if you see yourself in these statements:

- You don't see yourself growing in life.
- You think of yourself as not being good enough or smart enough.
- You never find anything good to say about yourself.

- You're always comparing yourself to others.
- You put up a barrier so no one can get close to you.
- You are suspicious about everyone.
- You can only point out the negative because all you see is negative.

If you answered "yes" or saw yourself in any of those statements, you need to change your mindset! As you start this new journey in your life, the first thing on the list is to change the way you see yourself. The way you do that is to take charge of what words you allow your mind to keep or reject. Only you can control what you allow in and what you throw out or keep. Whatever you pick is the mindset you will have. Take the pain of your past and use it to excel, not only in your present, but in your future as well.

"My trust and focus is on the Lord alone. He has declared me to be healed, therefore I am healed. He has declared my salvation: therefore I am saved." Jeremiah 17:14

What words did you speak to yourself this morning? Did your words give you enough fuel to make it through the day?

Your future is in the words you speak to yourself. Make the words you speak count. Don't allow the hurt of your past to hold you in bondage! Break free with the words you speak. Let your voice speak out loud and clear!!

Chapter 3

Forgive

"Oooh... I'm Telling"

Forgive! Yes, that's the word of the day! I'm going to talk to you about forgiving and how important it is. I'll discuss the effects of forgiveness, the changes it brings to you and others around you and the freedom that comes with it. There are <u>not</u> different levels of forgiveness. You can't halfway forgive someone. You have to be all in or all out; both feet have to be grounded and committed for you to forgive. The first step is to make the decision that you do not want to hold on to the offense anymore. You must make up your mind to release the stronghold off your heart and that you will no longer let this burden keep you tied up. You are going to use keys you didn't even know you had to unlock doors to the prison where you have been. Forgiveness sets your soul free to move on in life! Forgiveness stops the control that person or persons has over your heart dead in its tracks. Your heart pumps blood throughout your body. That's why it is so important for you to forgive; if not, it will affect your entire body. If you skip forgiveness, you will miss your healing.

I want to walk you through my journey and how I had to come to grips with having to forgive some people in my life so that my life could move forward. When I had unforgiveness in my heart, my life was at a standstill. I couldn't move; it was like my feet were in cement. Sometimes I would wiggle my feet out of the cement and think I had broken away, but I would soon find out it was like bungee jumping; you jump but are sprung right back to where you started.

Forgiveness is like getting a brand-new house and new furniture for each room! Or like swimming in the ocean and comparing that mass of water to your life of freedom! So, make up your mind that you do not want to stay where you are, tied up with unforgiveness. Get ready to live your life in freedom and release all the hurt and pain of the past. Forgiveness is **not** an easy thing to do, but it's necessary. You can't skip over it. It's a big part of the process of taking your life to the next level. It's a place of humility and it's uncomfortable, frustrating, and annoying and you feel like it's not fair.

Ephesians 4:2 says: "With all lowliness and meekness, with longsuffering, forbearing one another in love."

This is what Ephesians 4:2 means to me: I have to let go of bitterness, rage, anger, brawling, and slander, and everything that goes with it, and choose instead to embrace kindness and compassion for the ones who abused me and be ready to forgive just like Jesus has forgiven me. I have to be true to myself, and everything I was hiding had to be brought out into the open and be transparent. When I did that, I experienced an inner strength I had never had; but once you are on the other side of it, you realize it was all worth it. Those feelings can't even compare to the freedom you feel when you are dancing in forgiveness! Forgiveness is for you, it's not for the other person! I know you have probably heard that before, but it's true!

AsWhen I was a little girl, my eight siblings and I piled around the huge fireplace and watched movies with my parents. I remember it was so cozy and warm, and my stomach would be full from dinner, and halfway through the movie, most of us would be asleep. I was one of those who went to sleep.

As I got older, I remember hating holidays like Thanksgiving and Christmas, when all my family gathered at my mother's house. I would put on a fake smile as I made my way around to each family member. When I got to the members of my family who had repeatedly raped me, it took everything I had in me not to slap the piss out of each one of them. Bitterly, I would give them a big hug and have a conversation with them but at the same time; I didn't like them, and I didn't like being around any of them. I was faking the whole time I was at my mom's house, with a little help of a glass of wine or two. It gave me the temporary fix to get through those times.

I have had many flashbacks of the times we went shopping with my parents. All nine of us had to stay in the car. As soon as they left for the store, I had to use the bathroom really badly. My siblings encouraged me to get out of the car and go to the bathroom. All I heard was, "Hurry up and go; you'll get back before they do. We won't tell them you got out of the car." So I got up enough courage to get out of the car and ran fast as I could so I would get back before my parents. I made it! My parents had not gotten back yet! I was so happy. I grabbed the door handle to get in the car and it was locked! All I could see was my siblings with their mouths open, laughing and pointing their fingers at me as

I stood outside of the car crying begging them to unlock the door before my parents got back. I rewound that day in my mind over and over again and saw their laughing faces. When my parents got back and found me outside of the car, I got my butt torn up as my siblings watched and laughed. The saddest thing about it was that the ones who raped me were laughing the hardest.

Incidents like this were stopping me from my own freedom. I would not live in the present because I was stuck in the past. It was like buying a new car while the old car was at home in the driveway, but instead of me driving my new car, I was letting someone drive the new one and I was still driving my old car; one that was all beat up and raggedy, leaking oil, barely making it. Why? I couldn't just forgive those who had done wrong, and what I got out of it was that I wasn't able to go on with my life because I chose not to forgive. I didn't want to turn off the hurt of the past. I allowed myself to be tainted by someone who had wronged me in my past, dictated my present, and interfered with my future.

I was stuck on being hurt, and my present was being buried alive. I chose to stay hurt and you know what they say: "Hurt people hurt people." That is so the truth! I am a living witness! I wasn't happy, and I didn't want anybody else to be happy, either. Anger would arise within me, and I did not want to have anything to do with forgiveness because I was feeding anger, and it was overweight and getting heavier. As long as I allowed anger to have a foothold, nothing was going to change. As a child, a piece of me was taken every time they climbed on top of me; I felt like I had no control. But as an adult, I was in control. I had a choice. I could carry around this anger or I could forgive them. But honestly, anger felt better. I would tell myself, "You should be angry. You didn't deserve what they did to you. Stay angry as long as you want." I didn't realize that it was damaging me and my life in so many ways. The anger was not only against the ones who took my virginity but with my parents as well. They were supposed to protect me from hurt and harm, and they failed me. I had flashbacks of my childhood for most of my adult life. I held this anger for so long that it was a part of me; that's why it was hard to shake it off. But I tell you that <u>one day</u> a choice had to be made. I was tired and exhausted. The weight of anger is heavy and it affects your emotions, relationships, drive for life, health, mindset, and lifestyle, and it feels like your life is stagnant. I wanted change in my life, and I had the power to change it. So, **I decided** to forgive all those that had hurt me and **I chose** to forgive my parents so **I** could move on with my life. The key words here are **I decided, I chose,** and **I could**. It all started with me wanting to forgive so that I would become a new person, so that I could be a happy person, and so that I would be set free from anger. Unforgiveness was eating me alive! I was trapped, confined, I could only move so far. I was stuck, locked in. But, I had the key to unlock the door to let myself out. I could have freed myself a long time before I did, but the good thing is that I'm free now! I don't concentrate on how long I was confined by unforgiveness. My focus is on living a life of freedom and knowing it's my choice. YOU have the control to free yourself and forgive those that hurt and abused you in the past. Like I said earlier, I felt good being angry. Don't be deceived! It feels much better living a life of freedom.

I still remember when I made a choice to forgive. I had an abortion. It was my first pregnancy and I felt so guilty right after the procedure. I could not forgive myself. I felt confined within my mind, and I started hating myself. I didn't trust anybody, and I wouldn't let anyone get close to me. I had built a wall around me. I didn't go outside of that wall, and I didn't let anyone in. But when I gave birth to my second child, as soon as I saw his face, I forgave myself because I had a second chance to do the right thing and it made me think about the people who abused me and my parents, whom I thought should have protected me. Didn't they deserve a second chance, too? At that moment, I forgave them all. After that, wow, did my life forever change. I was on my way to live in purpose and in freedom! Anger no longer had a leash around my neck to lead me around like a dog. But it was a process.

The first step was to make a choice to forgive myself. After forgiving myself, I forgave others. Once I did that, I started going at life in a whole new way. One thing that worked in my favor was that I was in a different country, and that gave me time to work out some things in my life such as humble myself before Abba Father and let it all go. I still had a memory of the abuse, but I would not let it consume my life. I had to go back to my brokenness with forgiveness, not with anger. You must go back and visit that hurtful place, that broken palace. If you don't deal with it in a place of forgiveness, it will lie dormant until a circumstance or a person triggers it to come alive and it will continue in your life. But once you forgive, you start walking and talking differently. Your conversations will change. People who are close to you will see a new person in you. A lot of the time, we hold unforgiveness in our heart and it's tucked way back there and we don't even know it's there. I had to sit down with a piece of paper and pen and just ask, "Abba Father, is there anyone in my heart that I haven't forgiven?" Don't be in a rush. It might take some time; names may come up while you are sitting there, then some may come while you are driving or just lying in bed. Be patient. It is worth the wait. Freedom changes your life for good!

When you live a life of freedom, you stop criticizing and finding fault in yourself. You start focusing on serving others and less on yourself. Unforgiveness is like an untreated wound. When a wound is not treated, it becomes infected. It can spread throughout your body and once it gets into your bloodstream, in some cases, it can lead to death. Unforgiveness can affect your lifestyle. Ask yourself, "How do I know if I have truly forgiven this?" You know if you truly forgiven someone by what comes up in your heart when you hear that person's name in a conversation. What comes up in your heart? Anger, resentment, retaliation, bitterness? If you haven't forgiven, some emotions like this will come up. On the other hand, if you have truly forgiven the person, you can be around them and even have a conversation with them, but you must have boundaries. You can remember what they did, but the difference is that you won't let it consume your life.

Forgiveness is letting go of the past. I still remember what they did to me. I can't change what happened in the past, but I chose to forgive. When you don't forgive it stops you from growing; you are stuck in the past. But when you forgive, it pulls you out of the quicksand of bitterness and brings you into the place of freedom to love yourself. When you start loving yourself, it opens so many other doors in your life such as letting down all the walls you have been building to protect yourself from the outside world. Once you start opening yourself up and walking freely and upright, you will take off the mask you have been wearing for years. Your outsides were looking good but your insides were infected.

First, you have to examine yourself. Forgiveness is from the heart, not your head. If you try to forgive someone from your head, it will not work, it will not be genuine. Search your heart. Check your heart for unforgiveness. Your emotions will let you know if there is unforgiveness in your heart. Once you identify the unforgiveness, in your mind go back to that place and time where the abuse happened. Name each person who hurt you in any way. Say it out loud. "I forgive _____. (name(s)." It may take two days or weeks if there were some people you didn't even know you had unforgiveness for in your heart. When you open your heart and search and examine yourself, you are going to stir up some things in your heart. You don't have to be in that person or persons' presence to forgive them. Tell yourself you deserve a life of freedom. Freedom to love fully and have the relationships you are supposed to have.

Unforgiveness was robbing me of my peace of mind. But you have the power to change your emotions for the good, and forgiveness will do that for you. Don't wait for someone else to do it for you: Choose your own destiny. The truth of the matter is if you allow unforgiveness to fester in your heart, it will affect every area of your life. Things in your life will change. It's like being on a merry-go-round: You're moving but not going anywhere. When I made the first choice to forgive myself for killing my unborn child, that was the start to my healing and peace in my life. I started loving to the fullest. Go back to the place you were hurt, call out their names. It is important to say their names out loud; words are so powerful. Say <u>out loud</u> how they hurt you. Continue to speak out loud, say how they hurt you. Remember: This is not for the people who abused you, this for you and for the next generation! It's for your children and for their children. You can even go as far as to mentally go where the hurt took place and remember what you were wearing. Speak out loud anything you can remember. If you don't have a place you can be alone, whisper it. It's not about the volume.

Here is an example: Call their names and say, "I FORGIVE YOU (name) _____ FOR _____(abuse)_____. I let it go. I'm going to release all the things you did to me, and/or what you said about me, and I'm moving on with my life. I'm not going back to the place of hurt and unforgiveness! When it tries to come back, I'm going to remind myself of this day (speak the date) _____. This is the date I released it and let go of depression, bitterness, anger, impulsiveness, sickness, and/or allowing someone else to have power over my emotions. I choose the life of freedom, peace, a life of loving myself, a life of good relationships, a life of a positive mindset, a life of love, and a life of knowing my purpose and walking in it."

Yes, you can have that kind of life, just like me! The question is, are you ready for a positive change in your life? You are the only one who can make that choice. Once you decide that you are tired of carrying the past on your back and you make the choice to forgive, the process will begin, and you will have freedom like you have never known. You will have a new mindset; you are going to look at life with a new light. You will realize that you were walking around in the dark. You will have a brand-new walk, and you are going to realize that you were walking with a limp. As for the person or the persons who abused you, you will start praying for them. Yes, it's true! You will walk in true freedom; you will be passionate for those who abused you. Compassion with boundaries: I will talk more about boundaries in the next chapter. So, ask yourself, do you want to be confined to the past of hurt? Or do you want to start a brand-new life of freedom and take charge of emotions by living a life of FORGIVENESS? Ask yourself right now. Are you walking around with unforgiveness in your heart? Only you can answer that. If so, get a piece of paper or your phone. You can have a forgiveness release party right now. Ask yourself, do you have any unforgiveness in your heart? Ask Abba Father to search your heart. You know why He has to search your heart, because we hide things in our heart by not dealing with the issues. We think that if enough time passes, the hurt of the abuse and everything and everyone that goes with it will miraculously just disappear. Not true! You will walk through life with unforgiveness tucked back in your heart until something triggers it to show its ugly head. The trigger can come from the mention of someone's name, a place, a smell, a song, a memory, or even a thought. Forgive as quickly and completely as God forgave you.

"Regardless of what else you put on, wear love. It's your basic, all-purpose garment. Never be without it!" Colossians 3:13

Don't hold on to unforgiveness you have to forgive those who hurt and abused you. No one is worth your peace.

I hated the holidays because I would see the people who had abused me, and I would pretend like everything was good but it wasn't good, not even close.

Unforgiveness was weighing me down so badly, I couldn't even walk straight. I was so heavy with anger, I could not wait for that holiday to end! I tried my best to stay clear of them. But every time I turned around, they were right in my face. I was so tired at the end of the day. I'm here to let you know that carrying around unforgiveness is heavy! It takes a lot of energy. But I also remember the first time going to my parents' house as a free person: I had forgiven them all and was walking in freedom. I felt so wonderful! No more anger or rage. With help from the Lord, I was free from the unforgiveness that held me in captivity for years. I was discharged from rage, anger, isolation, fear, numbness, guilt, shame, and self-blame! I had been justified and redeemed! The layers of self-sabotage were pulled back and removed. My peace was present, and I loved the company.

"A true son and permanent member of the family, Therefore, since Jesus the true Son, became my substitute, I truly have been set free!" John 8:36

I was living the life of freedom! You can, too!

"God has promised me peace in this life. His salvation is always near to me and his glory resides with me forevermore. I will not forfeit this right by returning to the folly of my old ways." Psalm 85:8-9

I will not put myself back into prison. I love my freedom!

Forgiveness releases you from your pain and hurt from the past. Forgive and free yourself. Forgiveness is a big part of living a life of freedom. You are in control of what happens in your life because of the decisions you make. And the best decision you will ever make is the choice to forgive those who have hurt you so that you walk through life with peace and keep your focus on love and loving others.

When you forgive, you gain so much! For a long time, I thought if I forgave, it was a sign of weakness, but I found out it was the complete opposite. I gained inner strength by letting go of anger, rage, hate, and pain. I gained so much more. I opened the door to peace and compassion.

Ask yourself this question. "When I think of a person or persons who have hurt me or maybe someone brings up their name or names, what thoughts come up?"

Chapter 4

Stay In Your Lane

"Oooh... I'm Telling"

How can you accept who you are and all the triumphs and disappointments that come with being abused? You start by learning how to love yourself and not comparing yourself to others. You need to accept who you are because there is only one you. Abba Father formed you in your mother's womb. He chose which womb to put you in, He picked your mother and your father, and He knew exactly what He was doing. There is only one you, and you only have one life. Make up your mind that you are going to stay in your lane because the purpose of your life is to love God, yourself, and others. You were made to pour into others; that's why it's so important for you to be comfortable with who you are.

"I am fearfully and wonderfully made, and God is very proud to call me His child. My thoughts of myself are pure and positive. I know that I am a very special and unique individual with a grand purpose and destiny in this life." Psalm 139:14

When you compare yourself to someone else, it's like you are questioning God.

You may be walking, running, skipping, hopping, or sitting, the only thing you need to make sure of is that you STAY IN YOUR LANE! Don't run because someone else is running; it may be their season to run. God might have you in a season of walking, but don't step out of your lane and into someone else's: Embrace who you are and enjoy the season where God has you.

"My words bring healing to all who are touched by them, they are a tree of life, with limbs branching out and roots spreading within, forming an impregnable fortress of God's glory in this earth." Proverbs 15:4

Growing up, we went on vacation to Texas every year. My mom and dad met in California but they were both from Texas, so when we went to Texas, we got to see both grandparents. It was always a great time driving to Texas. I loved road trips. We stopped on the way and got snacks, and stayed overnight in a hotel. Just getting away from home for a few weeks was great, and once I got to Texas, things would change for me. First stop was my grandmother's, my mom's mother's house. We stayed for a few days and spent most of the rest of the time at my daddy's parents' house.

The reason things changed for me was because I felt overlooked as a young child. I was not told I was cute or pretty; no positive words were spoken to me. I probably wouldn't have noticed if it weren't for one of my siblings getting all the praise and compliments while I just stood there as if I were invisible. Don't misunderstand: I had amazing grandparents. But, let me tell you about my Papa. My sweet grandfather was the biggest reason I loved going to Texas every year.

He will always have a special place in my heart. He was the most loving, kind person I have ever known. My Papa was a pastor, and we went to church with him while on vacation, and afterward, my parents and siblings and grandmother would return to the house for dinner. My grandmother was an awesome cook. But after church, my Papa would go visit the sick and shut-ins and I would ask him if I could tag along. He always said, "Yes baby, you can come with Papa." We went down long, bumpy dirt roads deep in the Texas woods. He'd get out and I would be right there with him. He always made me feel safe, and I was so proud to be with him! He introduced me as his baby "Gigi." My Papa always acknowledged me at every house we stopped. I would say to myself, "I hope this is not the last house," as I did not want it to end. I could go visiting with him all day. I loved my sweet, sweet grandfather.

So, getting back to why I didn't enjoy time during our Texas vacations. Like I mentioned before, my mom and dad had nine children. Five of us are each a year apart, and I'm the youngest of that five. My sisters got so much praise from my Texas family. They told my sisters how pretty they were, and I was standing right by them, but it was like I was invisible. If they thought I was pretty, they kept it a secret from me. I don't blame my sisters for getting compliments; all my sisters are beautiful. They had long hair and their skin was lighter than mine. It is sad but true, I grew up when older people preferred lighter children, and I still think some feel the same way today. It didn't help at all on how I viewed myself as my self-esteem was not great anyway because of sexual abuse.

I would ask God, "Why don't I have long hair, and why is my nose flat, and why are my lips full?" How dare I question God about his masterpiece! He did not make a mistake when He made me or you. I didn't know that then, but I know it now! I tell my children and grandchildren no one stood in a "nose" line and said to God, "I want that nose" or got in a "hair" line and said to God, "I want that texture of hair." It doesn't work like that. God knew what He was doing when He put you together. When you were in your mother's womb, He was in charge.

I felt invisible most of my childhood. I can tell you today that I work with what I have. I am not saying that I don't have my days and sometimes weeks when I struggle with something. It could be my weight or lack of confidence, but the fact is I don't stay in that place. I encourage myself now. I love myself. I tell myself, "You're smart, intelligent, creative and funny." I pour positive words into myself, and it works! Everyone likes to be praised or admired, but guess what: You are not going to have people in your face all the time giving you compliments. That's why it's so important to admire yourself. It's not being conceited; it's about just knowing who you are and who made you. For example: You go to work everyday, and everyday you get a compliment from at least one person. But for some reason you go to work on a certain day and realize at the end of the day no one has given you a compliment. You may start thinking to yourself, "Was something wrong with me today? I didn't change my hair! Am I gaining weight?" You are second-guessing yourself because you are living off other people's compliments.

Instead, start before you leave the house. Look at yourself in the mirror and say to yourself, "You sure do look good today! You're going to have an awesome day today." Then if you get any compliments that day, they're just extra. What you think about yourself counts far more than what others think of you. What you think about yourself is what others will think about you. It all starts with you!

I started thinking of myself in a positive way instead of comparing myself with other people or wishing I lived in a different city or had a different family, etc. I started focusing on what I could do. I asked, "How can I better myself?" I set my eyes on my goals. I found out when I started shifting my attention on how I could be a better me, something really amazing happened. I stopped comparing myself to others and started looking for who I could help. When I stopped trying to get in someone else's lane instead of staying in my own lane, my whole way of thinking changed. This is how I looked at the situation: I love shoes, and Abba Father has blessed me with shoes. I use my shoes to make it clear to me that everybody has different seasons and events in their lives. Everyone is not in the same season. Just because you see somebody wearing six-inch pumps, it doesn't mean you need to buy six-inch pumps. What season are you in? In your season or your journey, you may be wearing tennis shoes. You may be in a different season in your life; you have to stay in your lane. Don't compare yourself to anyone; your journey is yours. It took years for me to realize it all starts with me knowing who I am, and not with what happened in my past. The real root cause was me. I had held myself back all these years. But now I have successfully survived and conquered negative thinking about myself.

"Jesus is the true vine and my father is the master gardener. I (your name _____) am a branch of the true vine. If I am not bearing fruit, my father will

prune away at me (cleansing and training me) until I do. He makes me what I am — joyfully molding and forming me, until I continually increase and bear richer and more excellent fruit." John:1-5

When I stay connected to the true vine, it keeps me in my lane.

I have fresh confidence and renewed inward determination to think good of myself. This is how I rise above other people's opinions of me. When I was emotionally unhealthy and broken, I lived off of what people said about me, good and bad. When it was good, life was good for me. But when it was bad, life was pretty miserable for me because I allowed someone else to come into my lane. Don't get me wrong, I think everyone likes compliments, but I can't allow other people's compliments to consume me. Be sure you are the first one to give yourself a compliment, and the ones you get after yours are icing on the cake or just extra. The key is to make time to spend time with yourself. Make a date with yourself. Put it on your calendar, and make sure you show up for the date. The more time I started spending with myself, the better I got to know me. At first I did not enjoy it at all, but the more I started hanging out with myself and Abba Father, the more things started to become clear to me. I had to accept all of me — the sexual abuse, the family I was born into, the mistakes I made, my physical appearance and my insecurities. I HAD to be true to myself, and I had to love myself regardless. I had to be comfortable with who I was to "stay in my lane" and stop comparing myself to others to make me feel good. I had to stop comparing because it is so exhausting, and it will consume you. I believe it's not a good place to be. When you stay in your own lane, you will start to look at yourself in a different way. You will start seeing something in yourself. Instead of seeing things as good and bad or looking to find fault in others, you start to self-check and find ways to better yourself. Starting to work on myself changed how I viewed others. My abusers look different to me now that I no longer have to pretend to be someone else when I am around them. I was not OK with what they did to me, but I looked at the situation differently. I changed my mindset. My grandfather always had kind words to say about me. I didn't realize the positive effect it had on my whole life. That's why it's so important to STAY IN YOUR LANE. It's your life, and you only have one. Everyone has someone who looks like you or favors you in some way, but the truth is there is no one in this world that is exactly like you or me!

There are some things in your life you can control and some things you can't but at the end of the day, you are still who you are and who God made you to be. The you that is good enough, that one who knows no matter what or who tries to stop you, you will just keep walking in your lane. If circumstances try to tie your hands up, you keep walking. When family members spread lies about you, pray hard for them and keep walking. Even when you sabotage yourself, forgive yourself and keep walking. Learn to embrace everything about you because there will never be another you! And remember your life is for you and you alone to live. Pour into someone else's life. You only have a short time here, so don't let someone else's wrong destroy the time you have on this earth.

"Yet you do not know what tomorrow will bring — what your life will be! For you are like vapor that appears for a little while, then vanishes." James 4:14

You choose to listen to what speed God is telling you to go in your lane. God is in control when you stay in your lane. You don't know when your journey — or lane — will end. You have to live your life free from unforgiveness, comparison, bitterness, and hatred. The problem I had was covering up my pain and hurt from the abuse by not staying in my lane. I always had a competitive mindset. I always had something to keep me busy and always found a reason not to spend quiet time with myself. I was in everybody else's business — or everybody else's lane — because I didn't want to deal with my own hurt. I kept it inside, I compressed my pain, and it accumulated over the years. Instead of using my time and energy to deal with my issues, I was always up in someone else's stuff.

Once you get in your lane and stay there, you will start to discover and identify the root of what's driving your emotions. After that, you will be able to stop and deal with each area in your life you need to work on. When you get to this point, you will start to see why you have been stagnant in some areas. When you are stagnant, it's like when water is not moving: There is an unpleasant smell. That happened the same way to me. When I allowed the hurt and the pain of the abuse to linger in my heart, my attitude started to stink, and even my facial expressions showed the world what was really going on inside of me. As you continue to walk in your lane, you are going to start dropping "weight" that you have been carrying for years, and you will realize how valuable you are and that Abba Father did His best work when He made you.

When I look back over the years, it wasn't people that were holding me back, it was *me* holding me back. I allowed my negative thoughts to sabotage my growth. It is all up to you to get in your lane and stay there. No one has the ability or the power to put you in your lane and to keep you there but you. It's not easy to stay in your lane because there are so many distractions. It is so easy to get in someone else's lane (business) and not deal with your own. Remember: You are the only one who should be in your lane. Your lane was made only for you. It's not a two-lane street, it's one lane — your lane — and it's just for you. Why? Because you are one of a kind. The abuse you endured just shaped you into the magnificent person you are today! You are still here. You have not given up on yourself. I know this because you are reading this book, and when you finish it, you are going to be so much more enlightened and amazed at how resilient you are. You'll know that you have so much strength and power inside you that was just waiting for you to turn the key and start driving to your destiny and true purpose. Don't allow the hurt and the pain of your abuse to drive you into someone else's lane, go after somebody else's destiny, or walk in someone else's shoes because of the lies others have told and the lies you have told yourself.

IT'S TIME FOR YOU TO WALK IN YOUR OWN SHOES IN YOUR LANE. Yes, you can; yes, you will! To validate is to acknowledge and accept a person. You are the first person to validate yourself because Abba Father has already validated you and what He said is far above what others think of you and what you think of yourself. Those thoughts must agree with what He says, because Abba Father has the first and the last word. On the other hand, invalidation means to reject, ignore, or judge. When you think of yourself, do any of these words come to mind? Do you know your worth? Do you know your value? When you look in the mirror, what words do you come up with? Are there negative words than positive words?

35

Well, let's do it right now! Go get a mirror. Take a minute to look at yourself and write down all the words that come to mind. Make sure these are your thoughts only, not what others have said. Write down every word that comes up. On another piece of paper, make two columns, one for positive words and one for negative words. Put down all the words you wrote down earlier in one of those columns. What side wins? This exercise will give you insight into what you think about yourself. Don't be hard on yourself. After you finish reading this entire book, do this exercise again and you will see you have a whole new mindset in the way you think about yourself.

Remember: Life is so much more enjoyable when you are you and not trying to be like or act like someone else. Stop hiding behind your pain and hurt and start loving you. Being confident and content in being you, you will be staying in your own lane. The abuse you endured does not define who you are; it's just a small part of your journey. Don't allow that one event in your life to keep you from becoming the best you can be or becoming the awesome person that you are! Use that awesomeness to help someone along the way. You can't remain in the hurt and pain; there are people waiting for you to help them reach their destiny! Ready, set, go! Stay in your lane. A life of fulfillment awaits!

"Have no cause for fear, for my God is with me. I will not be dismayed, for God is my Father and He has promised to never leave me, nor forsake me. He strengthens me and assists me in every circumstance, He upholds me with His righteous right hand so my victory is made certain." Isaiah 41:10

My oldest sister, Valerie, is so amazing in so many ways. I have always looked up to her. She has a style of her own, from the way she does her hair to the outfits she wears. God has blessed her with the gift of fashion. Not only that, she has so much wisdom that people just love being in her presence. We are nine years apart. I remember when I was young, I watched every move she made. I watched when she put on her makeup and did her hair. I loved everything about her. I wanted to be just like her when I grew up. She could not do any wrong in my eyes. But as I got older, I realized that it was unhealthy to compare myself to her. She is amazing to this day! But I had to start walking in my own lane. I had to discover that I had my own lane, and the way I did that was to look within myself and see the gifts and talents God had given me. The same God that knit her together in our mother's womb knit me together, too! He formed my inward parts, too. Praise God. He didn't forget about me, and He did not forget about you, either.

"Though the mountains be shaken and the hills removed, God's love for me will never fail and His covenant with me will not be taken away." Isaiah 54:10

I realized that God loves me. He made me and He did not make any mistakes. He knew exactly what He was doing when He knit me together in my mother's womb!

So yes, Lord yes, to your will in my life. Embrace you. Not parts of you, *all* of you! God can handle all of you: the good, the bad, and the ugly. You and I are made in His image. He made you and me. Just give Him permission to help you by surrendering to Him.

"Give Him free reign to increase within you and take the lordship over your life. Let him become the chief executive who will guide you in all that you set your hand to do." John 3:30

Do you want to go on this journey called life solo? Or have almighty God as your friend, protector, and the lover of your soul? It's your choice.

Chapter 5

Take Off The Mask

"Oooh... I'm Telling"

Just be yourself, come as you are, it's OK. Stop pretending. It is so much easier to be yourself. When you wear a mask, you are covering up the real you and allowing fear to drive you to be somebody you're not. Fear stops you from discovering the truth about who you really are. The reason I was wearing so many masks was because I was hiding behind my pain. The pain from my past was choosing the mask I wore for that day or month, and it would depend on where my life was and the current events. I felt safe behind the masks I wore. I would make it up as I went along. I would hide behind the lies and the pain and the hurt. I will talk about when I discovered that I wore a different mask everyday and how God started to peel away the layers of pain. And as the layers were being removed and my eyes were opened, I started to see the damaging effects of the sexual abuse. I was masking the hurt and pain I was afraid of.

"God will perfect what concerns me. Your mercy, O Lord, endures forever, do not forsake the work of your hands." *Psalm 138:8*

So I said to the Lord, "I give you all of me! LET THE HEALING BEGIN!"

And it did, although it was uncomfortable while he was peeling away the layers. I had to do my part as well. I had to confront a lot of demons.

I gave myself permission to take hold of who I was and embrace everything about all of it, the pretty and the ugly! And it was OK.

It is so important not to hide behind your pain. It's time to stop faking and be yourself. Just relax and be the best person you can be. It takes so much energy trying to be someone you are not. I wore my masks for so long and they were so tight on my face that they became a part of my life just like my family members. I wore my masks because I was so afraid and hiding behind the pain; and unsure of myself. I wanted approval from everybody. I wanted so bad to fit in. It was so exhausting trying to be anybody but myself. I had so many masks in my closet I became confused sometimes about which mask to put on that day, or even for the next 2 hours. It was such a lonely place to be in, always trying to fit in. No one really knew the real me; I didn't even know. Throughout my life, I met people that were really genuine. They did not stay long because I was dishonest. It was difficult for me to become friends with others because I was so focused on keeping up with the lies of the mask I wore that day that it was impossible for me to have true friendship. I was not telling the truth, and it was hard work keeping up with lies.

People who are truly genuine will see right through a fake person, which opened doors for me to be around the wrong people. I allowed myself to listen to all kinds of negative people, speaking profanity just to be accepted. Who or where I was determined the mask I wore. It was so exhausting. I had a mask for every area of my life, so basically my life was a big fake. My life was disguised as a masquerade party, but it was really more like a pity party.

The only one who was in attendance was me and my negative mindset. I had a mask for every relationship. On the outside, I was looking good. I had everything in the place. But the inside of me were layers and layers of pain that resulted in me wearing all the masks. I had no peace. I was so afraid of being me. I didn't like me because I didn't know me. So I wore on a mask to try to fit in wherever I was at the time.

Another mask I wore was getting into other people's business. I opened myself up to listening to endless problems that were not any of my business. I allowed the pain of my past to hold me prisoner, only to realize that my past was a lesson, not a life sentence.

1. I wore a "pity" mask. Poor little me; why did it happen to me?
2. I wore a "too much wine" mask. I drowned myself in wine trying to bury my pain and hurt.
3. I wore an "I don't care" mask. I made reckless decisions in my life and didn't care about the consequences.
4. I wore the "blame game" mask. I pointed fingers at everyone, even myself.
5. I wore a "church" mask.
6. I wore a mask when I was around my family.
7. I wore a mask in my first marriage.

Behind these different masks, I covered up sadness, insecurities, and fear. I was afraid of being me. I really didn't know how to be me. The pain of abuse had paralyzed me with pain and fear. The fear caused stagnation. My life was moving and my body was growing, but emotionally, I was still that nine-year-old girl.

I found out FEAR IS A LIAR!

- Fear told me I was all used up.
- Fear told me it was my fault.
- Fear told me I was not good enough.
- Fear told me no one would ever love me.

Fear is a liar. When I wore a mask, my focus was off, or on the wrong things. The company I kept was not genuine because *I* wasn't genuine. I wore a mask to cover up the real person I was so that was the kind of person and attracted people who did the same.

The pain was so deep, I didn't realize I was even wearing a mask. It was an integral part of my life that I didn't know the real me. I didn't know I was loved. I didn't know I was funny. I didn't know I was beautiful. I didn't know I was creative. I didn't know I was smart. I found out all of these things when I dealt with the pain and the hurt of my past.

First, I had to forgive my abusers. Then, I had to forgive myself and let myself off the hook in the sense of being responsible for the abuse. I had to disconnect from the people who abused me so I could heal. After I went through the healing process, I was strong enough to be around those who abused me and be myself around them and anyone else as well. I was walking in freedom! I was truly free to be me!

I view the world in a new way because I view myself in a new way. I delayed my healing and wore a mask because I would not let go of my pain of the past. I had to let go of the pain so I could start living in the present and run joyfully freely into my future. It's like when you exfoliate your face from the surface in scales or layers. That is what happened when I wore a different mask, but in the process of my healing, I had to deal with layers of pain and years of not letting go of it. I had to remove all of the dead skin, the layer of pain that was holding me hostage. I was exhausted. I had no peace at all. It was like I could not breathe. I had no freedom in my thoughts, no freedom in my walk, no freedom anywhere in my life. It seemed easier to pretend to be something that I wasn't, instead of dealing with the pain of my past.

My freshman year in high school was a fresh start for me because all of the friends I went to elementary and middle school with, attended a different school because the district changed zoning for my address. I went to school with new people, but I started fresh with masks and the lies that came with them. I made up so many lies and wore so many masks with my friends, teachers, and everyone. I was on a roll and once I started making up all the stories, I really didn't know who I was from day to day or week to week, and what I didn't know was that everyone was talking behind my back. They didn't know what to believe because I couldn't keep up with what I told and to whom.

When that four years came to an end, all hell broke loose. I was confronted by my lies and lost the two friends that I hung out with in my senior year because I couldn't be myself, but the truth was, I didn't know who I was. You would think I would've learned in high school, but I kept the vicious cycle going as an adult.

For years, I wore a mask because I was more comfortable being someone else than being myself. It was a big game for me, especially when it came to the opposite sex. I played games, wearing different masks, and I was believable. Well, I *thought* I was. In reality, I was really only fooling myself. I was tangled in a web of lies and the only person who could get me out was me. I had to stop living a fake life and start being truthful to myself because I deserved it.

I remember coming home from a Black History program at my church. We had a long weekend and had been in church the whole day. My boys and I were tired. My first husband did not attend church, so when we got home that night he had a look on his face that let me know something was not right. I asked him if he was OK, and he said, "I don't think so." The morning after taking my boys to school, I took my husband to the hospital. We were there all day. The doctor ran a battery of tests on him, and he had to spend the night in the hospital to have more tests run the next day. Eventually, we received the terrible news: My husband had colon cancer and had two or three years to live.

That hit me hard! My four bonus children were young adults. Our four biological sons were still at home, and ages 16, 15, 9, and 6. I could not find the words to tell them that their dad had three years to live. So, I pulled out another mask to wear: The Supermom mask.

A mom takes care of everybody. I took care of my husband and my sons and did it all without showing any emotion. I thought life would go on as usual, that we would beat this cancer and go on with our lives. I really believed in my heart that my husband would be healthy again.

Six months passed. My husband was undergoing chemotherapy treatments and getting weaker by the day. The holidays came, and I was so exhausted. I still had to go get Christmas presents for my sons and really didn't want to go alone. My husband knew by the look on my face that I was so exhausted, and he asked in a weak voice, "Do you want me to go with you?" I was pleasantly surprised! I said yes, that it would help me a lot. So we got in the car. I was so excited; it felt like things were normal again. However, minutes later, my husband turned to me and said, "I can't go. I'm too sick. I'm so sorry." I just looked at him and said, "It's OK. Thanks for trying."

I still didn't give up. I told myself he was going to get better and life was going to be just like it was before the diagnosis. I remember getting up early in the mornings before my sons and going to the hospital to bathe my husband because he did not want the nurse to do it. Then I returned home to get the boys off to school.

It was cold that morning in Dallas. My sons were out of school that day and my husband had an appointment later that morning. My plan was to take my husband to his appointment and come back and relax because I had taken a day off of work. The night before was different, but I didn't think much about it until later. I asked my husband if he wanted to take a bath that night He usually said no and washed up himself. But that particular night he surprised me and said, "Yes, I do want to take a bath." I asked him if he'd like me to help him, and he said yes.

That night in bed, he could not get comfortable. He tossed and turned the whole night. I asked him if he was hungry and he said yes. I got up to make him something to eat, not knowing it would be his last meal. That morning after I helped him get dressed, he was sitting in the living room with our sons watching TV and I was in the other room getting dressed. I heard one of my sons yell, "Mom, Daddy's eyes are rolling back in his head!" I ran into the living room, and my husband was unconscious. My oldest son and I walked him to the car because my husband told me not to call the ambulance if he could walk to the car. We got him to the hospital, and I had someone pick up the other boys from home. I called the rest of the children to let them know they needed to come to say goodbye to their father, and less than a year from when the doctor told my husband he had colon cancer, he passed away.

I was in shock. I did not believe he was gone forever or that I wouldn't hear his voice any more or see his smile. I remember walking out of the hospital and my youngest son, who was seven years old at the time, turned to me and said, "Mom, so when is Daddy coming home?" I could not answer him. Someone in my family pulled him to the side to explain to him that his daddy was gone from the earth.

I realized that from the time the sexual abuse started to that very moment, I had worn so many masks. I wore a mask that said everything was just fine with me. I wore the mask of fear and kept silent. When I was younger, I was so afraid to tell my parents — or any adult for that matter — about the abuse. I was afraid to stand up for myself. That fear was still present during my teens. I later started wearing the mask of self-destruction because I could not realize my value. Then I went off to college and discovered

I could manipulate the opposite sex in ways that could get me what I wanted (but let's be clear that I did not give up any of my goodies). I teased all day long to get what I wanted. And the problem was that when I picked up a new mask, I stored all the other ones. I wore whatever mask that "fixed" that particular circumstance. As I got older, I accumulated more masks.

At the time of my husband's passing, I was 36 years old and had a plethora of masks. And the collection was growing. That's when I made up my mind to do something about it, and my heart agreed. I began spending endless hours examining myself. When I first started this process, I hated being alone. I didn't like who I was. I didn't know who I was.

I had worn a mask for as long as I could remember. I allowed the heaviness of the pain and hurt to fester in my heart for years. I wore masks because of the pain in my heart. But let me tell you the good news of how I overcame and started living and stopped wearing a mask for every circumstance and every occasion that came into my life!

I was living an authentic life for the first time. The first thing I had to do was admit to myself that I was living a fake life and that I wasn't happy with it. I had to self-check. In other words, I had to be real with myself. You can't be real with anyone else until you become real with yourself. It's not going to be easy, but it is worth it. You have to come to grips with your weakness and strengths, know the difference, and be OK with both.

Your past will not stop your future. Your past will push you into your destiny. You must make up in your mind that you are one of a kind. In the grand scheme of things, the event only makes up 10% of your experience, and your response makes up 90%. Change is hard but not impossible.

When I stopped comparing myself to others, life started getting better. Begin with the exercise of looking at yourself in the mirror and just loving yourself. I really felt foolish when I did this for the first time, but guess what? The more I did it, the easier it got. It got to the point that it was hard for me to pass by any mirror and not say an encouraging word to myself.

You must start seeing yourself as God sees you and know that you have purpose on this earth. He allowed you to still be here at this exact moment, reading this book at this time in your life. Look at your life as a movie. My sexual abuse was just one part of my life. It was not the end of my story or "movie." Don't allow your past hurt to direct your life. Yes, hurt had a brief scene or small part, but there are so many other scenes that overshadow it. Love yourself: The good, bad, strengths and weaknesses.

Words are so powerful. Your words come from your thoughts, and your thoughts come from your heart. It all starts with you realizing that God made you and loves you, and He doesn't make any mistakes! Believe it! Think it! Speak it! It works, I know, because it worked for me and it will work for you.

Winners never quit! You must keep moving. When you have a change of heart, your thoughts change. When your thoughts change, your words change. When your words change, your actions change. When your actions change, your environment changes. When your environment changes, your company changes. When your company changes, your life changes!

Don't let hurt and pain take up residence in your heart. Serve pain, hurt, and unforgiveness an eviction notice today. Yes, you can do this! This is your time. Knowing your true value will strengthen you in areas of your life. You may not feel valuable or loved, because you don't know your true value. True value = confidence in knowing that God loves you and you are the apple of His eye. You are His pride and joy. When you realize that Abba Father loves you, you will know your true value and you will walk with a quiet confidence. The word capable also comes to mind. Capable = the ability to do. I believe you are capable to perform, adapt; and that you are qualified, skillful, and talented. That's you!

Another word that comes to mind is the word intelligent. Intelligent = very smart, clever, ready, resourceful, smart, witty, exceptional, and creative.

You have to speak to yourself until you believe you are what you are speaking. Throw away all the masks you have been wearing and stop living a fake life. You are free to be who God called you to be, and that is victorious!! There is a difference between self-confidence and knowing your true value. For me, having self-confidence means relying only on yourself for everything you need. You think you can pull from within yourself and get whatever you need without asking anyone else for help or taking help from anyone. You have a mindset that you've got things under control as long as you have you and only you. You will be able to handle everything that comes your way.

I was only deceiving myself. The reality was that self-confidence only took me so far. On the other hand, knowing your true value is knowing that the Almighty God has a plan for your life. I didn't say you will understand everything that was going to happen in your life. I said He has a good plan for your life. That means that no matter what happens, good or bad, you are going to come out on top! But you have to do your part with letting the hurt and the pain of the past go. Not some of it, *all* of the pain and hurt and everything that comes with the pain and the hurt, such as unforgiveness and bitterness must go. We must clean out our heart and lay everything at the feet of Jesus.

Wearing different masks can be a deadly weapon in more ways than one. The mask makes you walk through life with blinders on your eyes. When you can't see, you bump into things and hurt yourself. The blinders will also make it difficult to tell who your real friends are. You miss out on opportunities. You become stagnant, like a body of water or an atmosphere of a confined space, having no current or flow and often having an unpleasant smell as a consequence. The unpleasant smell is your stinky thinking and negative mindset.

People wear so many masks. You must examine yourself and be truthful. I discovered all of my masks were covering up the hurt and the pain I didn't want to deal with or that was too painful to revisit. I wore a mask to mask my pain. When you make up your mind that you want change and you act on it, you will be on your way to getting rid of those masks for good, and on your way to living your life in truth!

Are you living in the hurt of your past? If you are living your life behind a mask, you are living a fake life. Only you know the answer to that question. Start today. Ready? Set. Go. Take off that mask! You have the power to do it. Let go of the pain of your past. Don't allow your abuse to hold you hostage and force you to pretend to be or act like someone that you are not. Remember this, when you hold on to the hurt of your past, you are suppressing your emotions and the need to wear the mask becomes stronger. Sometimes someone or something will trigger those masks or feelings and force you to react the wrong way! But it's time to live your life in freedom!

"I have no cause for fear, for my God is with me, nor will He forsake me. He strengthens me and assists me in every circumstance, and upholds me with His righteous right hand so that my victory is made certain!" Isaiah 40:31

That scripture tells me that the almighty God is with me when I fall. I don't have to pretend to be anybody. He will uphold me so that when I stop wearing masks, I am comfortable being who God made me to be. He made me in His image. Nothing or anyone can compare to Him.

Never allow your past to make you a prisoner in your present. It was a small part of your life, not a life sentence. Ask yourself the questions that no one else can answer but you:

1. Are you being true to yourself?
2. Have you truly let go of the hurt and pain of your past?

Once you start the healing process, don't surrender to the hurt and pain. Surrender to the truth. Surrender to the freedom of being you. Yes, you will stumble, mess up, get frustrated, and look and sound different, but start walking in your purpose and you will reach your destiny. All of these things are distractions. You have to keep moving forward while keeping you in mind. Clear your heart of unforgiveness so you can heal and start to hear what's being said without the filter of your pain. There's simply no stopping you! When you do this, there will be no more hiding behind a mask, and no more denying yourself the time to walk in your own path and be proud of your progress.

Move out of your comfort zone and be who you were meant to be! That is truly being yourself. When you wear different masks, you are masking your emotions. When you do that, you are denying yourself in so many ways. The words you speak to yourself can either defeat you or bring victory to your life. If you are saying to yourself, "I can't seem to get over that place in my life," you are speaking words of defeat. Victory will run away from you and self-pity will run toward you. Your words can be deadly or they can renew life. You can change your life when you change the words that come out of your mouth. You can't control what comes out of anyone else's mouth, but you do have power and control over what comes out of yours. So what are you going to choose: to stay in prison from the pain and hurt of your past, or to live a life of forgiveness and freedom? Your choice: Victory or defeat?

The biggest thing I want you to get out of this chapter is: Holding onto the hurt and pain of your past you will make you stagnant in your emotions and other areas of your life. Take off the masks so you can really hear what your heart is saying without the filter of your hurt and pain.

Ask yourself:

1. Are you being honest with yourself? Only you know the answer to that question.

You might as well be true to yourself because God knows all about it, and He loves you more than you can even imagine.

Chapter 6

Words

"Oooh... I'm Telling"

The words you speak shape your present as well as your future so that's why it's so important for you to choose them wisely. Your words can put you on top of a mountain or place you in a dark, deep hole just by simply speaking those events into reality. They are so powerful! You can talk yourself into your destiny or away from it. I did not realize the power of words. You can change your whole life with the words you speak from *your* mouth, it's right there under your nose.

- Are your words building up or tearing down?
- Are you using your words as a weapon or as a peacemaker?

Words have the power to get you out of bed in the morning or have you bed-ridden for months! In this chapter, I will share with you how I changed my life and the life of my children by choosing wisely and selecting the words I spoke.

"God has abundantly blessed me with good things of every kind. God created me to live and walk in dominion. The Lord has provided to me all of the

resources in the earth, All things are His and He has made me a steward of His riches in this earth" Genesis 9:1 and 3

Beware of the words that come out of your mouth. Once they leave your mouth, you have to deal with what comes next. Good or bad, whatever you spoke was your choice. Your words shape your world.

It's so important to know the words you speak. Those words are shaping your life. They create what kind of day you are going to have. They create what kind of people you invite into your life. They determine how you react in circumstances. Words play a big part in your life. Guard your mouth, and think before you speak. Where your life is today came out of your mouth! That is a hard pill to swallow for some of us.

When I realized that I had power in my tongue and the words that came out of my mouth, and that I controlled where my life would go, I was so excited! I said to myself, "It's that easy?" The next morning when I got up, I went to the bathroom, looked at myself in the mirror and said, "You are beautiful, Gisele." Then I started laughing. You know why I laughed? I didn't believe it. Now that's the hard part! I had to believe in what I was saying. I didn't believe what I was saying at first, but the more I spoke those words to myself, the more I started to see myself as beautiful.

Let your words be like water to a plant. Whatever you water will grow. I would say to myself, "I'm damaged for life because of the sexual abuse," or "I will never forgive the people who abused me." I was watering words like this into my life and they were growing. If you are saying words like this, you are allowing the wrong ones to grow in your life, too. These are the words you should be speaking out loud to yourself: "Yes, I was sexually abused, but that was only a part of my life. Yes, it's difficult, but I'm not going to surrender to the hurt; I'm going to keep moving forward until I reach my destiny." I started to change my vocabulary because the words I chose to come out of my mouth were orchestrating my life. If you want to know what's in your heart, start listening to the words you say. Don't allow other people's words to tell you who you are or where you should go. Don't accept lies! If it doesn't line up with what God's word says about you, don't sign for the package, it's not yours! Yes, that's what I allowed for years until I realized I was accepting the lies and giving someone else power over my destiny. I had the power right under my nose. The words that come out of my mouth are powerful! Words shaped my life. Words are like bricks. When you are building a house, you don't want to miss a brick. You have to lay each brick one by one and eventually, you will finish the house. Each day when I woke up, I had to start speaking words that encouraged me and lifted me up. Faith holds fast to the confession of your words. I was destroying myself by my own words. I had to stop telling lies to myself.

Proverbs 18:21 says, "The tongue has the power of life and death. The stakes are high. Your words can speak life or death."

That goes for the words you speak to yourself. You can build you up or tear you down!

I remember one morning I had been looking for a job for about a month. The words I spoke to myself that morning were, "Gisele, you are going to get a job today." I got dressed.

I had a plan to walk into this particular company. I was going to get an interview that day and be hired. While I was driving there, I spoke words of encouragement like, "You can do this. You are going to get this job today. Fear has to go, no fear today." As I approached the front door of the building, I spoke words of life over myself. I tell you, when I walked into that office, the words I had spoken to myself became alive in me! When I walked out of that building, I had been offered a job on the spot. I believe it was because the words I spoke became real. You become the words you speak. If you speak magnificence, you will be magnificent. What's your account balance? The words you speak are not in vain. The words you speak are like a bank account. You can have a balance of $0.00 or a balance of thousands. A $0.00 balance is the sum of all of the negative words I have spoken over my life for years plus the lies that others have spoken over my life and me believing the lies. I had a $0.00 balance because the words I spoke added no value to my life. When I realized that, I made up my mind that I needed to change and start to be very careful in choosing my words. When I did that, I started to deposit into my account words of encouragement, and words of empowerment, words that would take me to the next level in my life!

My account was growing, and I was building up my confidence. My account was no longer in the negative, meaning that my heart (account) was changing from emptiness to full of aspiration and optimism. You have the authority to deposit negative or positive words in your life account. When that abuse happened so early in my life, I was my own worst enemy. What I thought and spoke about myself was so negative because I didn't know my worth. I spoke words of defeat. My balance was $0.00, but when

I started speaking words of encouragement to myself, words of life, my account balance grew.

The more you speak positive words to yourself, the more you build your confidence. Even if you don't believe what you are speaking, keep doing it, and eventually you will believe what you are saying. When you are speaking the right words but you don't believe them yet, I call that "taking out a loan." You do not have ownership; you are just borrowing these words until you believe what you are speaking to yourself, but keep on speaking positive words. I will give you some examples that worked for me.

- You are beautiful.
- Gisele, you are one of a kind.
- You can do this because you are intelligent.

Verbal words of affirmation are powerful! When I first started speaking uplifting and encouraging words to myself out loud, I didn't believe a word I was saying. But I continued to do it, and eventually, I started to believe. My mindset changed. I looked at life with a new set of eyes. The way I walked changed. The way I viewed others changed in a positive way. My mind was not cluttered with piles of insecure thoughts that drove me to make wrong life decisions. The words that I spoke over my life helped to shape it. I was not walking through life with blinders on bumping into things, falling over cliffs, grabbing and inviting the people into my life who weren't supposed to be there. I used to just allow anybody into my life "just because." They served no purpose; they were just taking up space. I was drowning from the words I spoke. They were lies, and I believed the lies. The messed up thing about all that was, I was speaking words of death to myself! I didn't realize I was clearly burying myself alive with the words I was speaking to myself.

Things changed for me when I opened the eyes of my heart and realized that I was listening to the wrong opinions. I went to who made me, and He exchanged the truth about me for the lies. He showed me the great love He has for me. When God looks at me, all He sees are good things. He did not change His opinion of me after I was sexually abused. He made me in His image so that tells me I am beautiful. I went to who formed me in my mother's womb and I found the truth about who I really was. I stopped believing the lies. So, this is what I discovered. First, God created me in His image (image: a physical likeness or representation of a person, in the absence of the original stimulus.) There's more! I am fearfully and wonderfully made. Fearfully, when translated in Hebrew, means "with great reverence, heart-felt interest, and with respect to be unique and set apart." That's when I started giving myself permission to be me. I was made to be different. It's OK not to be like everyone in your family. You're valuable. You are loved. You are chosen. You are forgiven. You are a child of God!

He has put a crown with glory and honor on my head. I learned that I had the authority to speak words of greatness into my destiny. I had the power right under my nose all the time. After discovering all of this information, the next step was to speak what I was saying into reality, and to believe it. I started confessing words of encouragement in my life even when I did not believe them. You can confess what you don't believe, you just have to keep confessing until you believe. After you start to believe, your words will come alive! My life started to turn for the better. So, don't become frustrated when you initially change your words of defeat to words of encouragement. Keep speaking to yourself until you believe! I cannot tell you how long it will take until you start to believe because everyone is different. But I can tell you that it works!

As long as I can remember, I talked down to myself. I was my worst enemy. No matter what was going on in my life, I was defeated even before I started because my words paralyzed me. I remember I was in a program. I had about two months to study and memorize my lines, which I did. Just before I got on stage, I began talking to myself. "Why did you agree to do this? You know you do not do well in situations like this." Fear surrounded me. I was on stage by then. All eyes were on me. I just started making up words. I didn't sense at all. I didn't even look at the faces in the audience. It felt like I was on stage for five hours but in reality, it was only about three to five minutes. I had memorized my lines, but the words I spoke to myself dictated my outcome. Similarly, the words you speak shape your future. I realized that night, that it was my responsibility to determine how my life turns out. I hold the controllers of my destiny, and the words I choose to come out of my mouth are powerful!

I discovered my words can either be like bullets that kill my destiny or like a rocket that shoots up and pushes me closer to my destiny. I could have allowed the sexual abuse as a child to continue to shape my future, all because I didn't know my value, and the impact of the words I spoke to myself. I turned my life around when I changed my words.

Hebrews 13:6 says, "So that I can boldly say, The Lord is my helper and I will not fear what man can do to me."

Fear was driving this self-hatred BUT the Lord is my helper. He rescued me from myself! I started to discover what He thought of me and what He saw when He looked at me. I was blown away when I found out. It didn't matter what I thought about myself, or what anybody else thought about me, or that I was raped repeatedly at the age of nine. How He sees me never changes. His opinion matters because He was the one who put me together while I was in my mother's womb. He made me — and He made you! — in love. What God says about me and you are final. The words you speak shape your life.

Whatever words you choose to come out of your mouth … be ready for them to become reality. When my children were growing up, everyone would come downstairs for breakfast before school and one of my children would start speaking negatively. Before they even realized what was coming out of their mouth, it was too late. They looked right into my eyes and they knew what was coming. I told them to go back upstairs and start all over again, and this time, to choose their words wisely so they would have a good day. If you wake up complaining and angry and upset, more than likely you are going to have an unhappy day. So, if you focus on one occurring misfortune of events in your life and allow it to take command over the rest of your life, you will be giving up on yourself. Words are so powerful, but you hold the key to the power box. Words are powerful. Choose to be a power house.

"Through faith we understand that the worlds were framed by the word of God, so that things which are seen were not made of things which do appear." Hebrews 7:11

You have to speak out of your mouth what you want to appear in your life. You can change your world and the people around you by speaking words of life, words of encouragement, words that lift you up, and words that push you to the next level. Love on yourself with words. Speak to yourself. Don't compare yourself to others. You will lose every time, and you are insulting God when you do that. The fastest way you can get frustrated and down on yourself is by feeling sorry for yourself and starting a pity party. No one will attend but you and your enemies. The reason your enemies are there is because they want to keep you in the negative place you have allowed yourself to go to. Make sure your words are words of love, words of power, and words of life. Have the determination to take control of your words.

You have to treat negative words like a disease or an unwanted package and refuse to keep them!

The words you speak to yourself are a big part of claiming victory over abuse. Overcoming abuse has so many components and they all are very important, but the words you choose make a big difference in how you pull yourself out of the pit of hurt, shame, and unforgiveness. Take back your life with the words you speak quietly to yourself. Let every word you speak become a ladder you can use to climb out of that pit. Your life is a garden and your words are seeds. Whatever you plant will come up. So plant good words and your harvest will be a good one!

- Are your words building a high-rise or a shed? Words are powerful. Build a power house!

Chapter 7

Grace

"Oooh... I'm Telling"

In this chapter, I will walk you through my hurdles and down times, and explain how I tried to understand why my life could have gone in a different direction. I asked myself, "Why was I singled out to be raped at nine years old? Why was I even born into my family?" I know this is harsh, but I'm being transparent. I was so angry at my parents, the individuals who took my virginity at the age of nine, and upset at myself about all the bad decisions I made because I was walking around on this earth broken and unhealed. Fear grabbed at me from every angle. My emotions were everywhere. I dealt with guilt, shame, self-blame, anxiety, relationship problems, depression, negative thoughts about myself, feeling dirty and ugly, all of the above, and then some.

Through it all, God's grace had me surrounded the entire time. He had a good plan for me the whole time! In this chapter, I'm going to share with you how He poured His love on me and put me on the right path.

One morning I was in my bedroom, ugly crying so hard. I tried to stop, but the tears kept coming. I put my head in my pillow and started screaming into it. "God help. I don't know what to do. I don't know where to go. Please help!" Suddenly, I stopped crying, it got so quiet and then I heard a voice say, "Go read Psalm 32:8."

"I will instruct you and teach you in the way you should go; and I will guide you with my eye." Psalm 32:8

After reading that verse, the love I felt in the room was amazing! All of my fears and concerns were gone. I experienced a peace I can't explain. My life changed in a big way that day! The almighty God said He would tell me and teach me where to go, and on top of that, His eyes will be on me as I go. Wow! Hallelujah!

This is so important because there is a reason why I went through those highs and lows and made it! It was for you. I didn't know this early on. Being able to help others through the fire is one reason God allows us to survive tragedies in our lives. While I was going through the abuse, I was not thinking about it like, "Oh good, I'm going through all this hurt and shame to help someone that will go through this also." That was not the case at all. Thinking about someone else was the last thing on my mind. It was all about me, and "Why me, why didn't I speak up, why was I born, why am I in this family?" There were a lot of whys, and they were all about me. But in my journey to heal, I discovered it's not even about me. It took me awhile to swallow that giant pill of humility, and realize that while things were pretty bad, they could have been a lot worse.

For seven years, I worked as a mentor for middle school girls, ages 12 to 14. I traveled to a different school each day of the week, teaching a six-week course that covered different topics. My heart was so broken and hurt after leaving some of those schools, and in some cases the authorities had to get involved. There's one story that stands out to me. In the six weeks I was there, I built close relationships with the girls, some more than others. They knew I really cared and wanted the best for them. There was a 12-year-old girl who stuck around one day after class was over and all the other girls had gone. She said, "Can we talk?" I said "Sure!"

I was not ready to hear what I was about to hear. She told me that she was at her grandparents' house and had walked in on her 22-year-old uncle molesting her 6-year-old little sister. She grabbed her little sister's hand and took her to her mother. She was crying as she told her mother what she had walked in on. She was expecting her mother to react in a totally different way than she did. After she finished her story, her mom's response was, "Who else did you tell?" The girl said she was confused about her mother's reaction; she didn't even ask her little sister if she was OK. She answered her mother and said, "No one, you are the only person I told." Once they left her grandparents' house, her mom sat her down after her little sister went to bed and told her daughter that her grandfather had started molesting her (the mom) at a very young age and had gotten her pregnant, and that he did the same thing to her mom's sister, and the grandmother never said a word! She said after that day, she never looked at her grandparents the same way. I asked her, "How old is your grandfather?" She told me he was in his late seventies. That told me that this family secret had been kept for a long time. I thought it could have been a lot worse for me. I, too, could have gotten pregnant by my abusers, but the grace of God kept me. I was still in my pity-party stage and didn't yet realize that things could have been a lot worse. Abuse is a horrible ordeal to go through for anybody, but there is someone out there who is in a worse situation than you are.

I can also remember a story of another young girl. She was fourteen, and even before she started talking, her expression said it all. She was such a pretty girl. As she looked straight into my eyes, she was probably thinking, "Should I share my story or just keep it to myself?" She started off really slow and timid but once she got in the swing of things, there was no stopping her. She said her mom's boyfriend had taken the door to her room off and every time she took a shower he was in there, acting as though he needed to get something from the bathroom. That's how it started. He watched her get dressed while her mom was at work. One day, he picked her up from school and molested her when they got home. She told her mother and her mom put him out of the house, but she didn't call the authorities. She told her daughter not to say a word to anyone. One year later, the mother got back with this man and allowed him to move back in. The girl was so mad that her mother let him come back that she decided to get revenge. She began having sex with her mother's boyfriend right under her mom's nose.

This last story really broke my heart. This young lady was in the eighth grade for the second time. She was 15 years old and pregnant. We started talking about her plans to continue going to school after she had the baby. I can't recall how we spoke about the paternity of the baby, but she went on to tell me that he was 35 years old. I said "What?" and asked what her parents thought about the situation. She said, "I don't know where my dad is. My mom is a single parent and she doesn't care, because he pays all her bills." So basically, the mom was pimping her daughter out.

The reason I shared these stories is because all these girls were exposed to sex at a young age. All their parents let these girls down. The parents did not protect these girls. By the grace of God, I was in the position to help these girls come out of their abuse. At that time in my life, I was still trying to cover up the abuse from my childhood, and I was still feeling my own hurt and pain. God allowed me to love these young ladies and help them to escape!

"Thou hast granted me life and favor, and thy visitation hath preserved my spirit." Job 30:7

God kept my spirit. He stayed with me all the way. I had to really come to grips with that because I asked myself, "If God was with me the whole time why did He allow it to keep happening over and over again?" Now I understand. I know ...

"... that in all things God works for the good of those who love him, who have been called according to this purpose." Romans 8:28

God had a plan and a purpose for my life. What my enemy meant for evil, God turned around for my good. I'm writing this book to help someone who has been abused. All of my journey has been for my good. At times it didn't look like it, and didn't feel like it was for my good, but God had a perfect plan all along.

"Lord, by his favor he has made my mountain to stand strong; He did not hide his face when I was in trouble." Psalm 30:7

He allowed me to stand strong through my abuse. He did not hide His face when I was being abused, so that I could not only help those girls out of their situations, but to stand strong so I could write this book! God is at work in all things. You have to surrender everything to Him. He already knows anyway; He is waiting on you. You must see yourself doing more, gaining more, and being more. And the only way you can do that is to see yourself the way God sees you. Whatever your predominant focus, prioritize its existence in your life. Focus on negative, and that's what you are going to get. Focus on the positive, and that's what you are going to get! Negative or positive, what's it going to be? It's your choice. If you don't like the way your life is going, change the way you think. You can choose to focus on the abuse and how many ways it was wrong. You can play the blame game and say, "Somebody should have protected me. Where were my parents? Why did this happen to me? What did I do to deserve this?" You can come up with so many reasons. I know, because I have come up with many myself. Life is a result of your focus. You have to change your focus. Don't dwell on the past. Learn from it. Grow from it.

"God's grace is sufficient for me! God's grace is all that I need to stand in perpetual victory in this life, for His strength in me is made perfect in my weakest. Therefore, even when I am weak, the strength and power of Christ rests on me." 2 Corinthians 12:9

I was at a weak place in my life while I was on my back being sexually abused, but God's strength made me perfect in my weakness, and that's what I choose to focus on: Victory over abuse by God's grace.

"By his sacrifice, He has made me complete — absolutely perfect in God's eyes and it's my job to do the same kinds of things that he did in his earth walk." Luke 6:40

As I look back over my life, I realize that God was with me the whole time.

It was so hot in the desert the day my cousin asked if I wanted to play tennis with her. I thought about it for a minute because it was so hot, but she convinced me to go. After I got in the car, she said, "Hey cuz, I have one stop to make and then we'll go play tennis." We pulled up to a yellow colonial-style house and I asked her who lived there. She said that she was doing a favor for a friend and was going to comb his little girl's hair for him. "Come in with me," She said. "We'll only be here for about 10 minutes." So we knocked on the door and went in. There were two children, a boy and a girl. The children's father was an attractive older man, and as my cousin did the little girl's hair, all of his attention was on me. Maybe because I was wearing a cute little tennis outfit, but he was checking me out and asking me questions. I felt really awkward because he was acting like he and I were alone in the room. I was saying to myself, "I know this old dude is not trying to talk to me." My cousin finally finished the little girl's hair. I was so ready to go. I jumped up so fast, but not fast enough. The old dude walked us outside and just before I reached for the car door handle I heard him say, "Can I take you to lunch?" The first thing that came to me was "Hell no!" I was eighteen years old and he was in his thirties ... and had two children! But instead, I said, "Sure why not?" What was I thinking? Once we got back in the car my cousin said, "Are you serious?" I said, "Girl, there's no harm in going to get something to eat with him." I was in my second year of college.

He picked me up after my last class. He was a nice guy. On that first date, he let me know he had two more children who lived with his mother in Texas! I was speechless. He tells me, "I want to be straight up with you." So everyday after that first date, he picked me up. We got married a year later. Yes, I married that old dude. God's grace kept me even in that decision. I was not ready to be anybody's wife or mother; I was a broken soul then. I was not healed from being abused. I didn't know what I was getting myself into, but I found out really fast. God was always with me. I didn't know that then, but when I look back over my life, I know He was right there. I thought I was taking control of my life by getting married because so much was taken from me. I wanted to get over the feeling of guilt, and the numbness, anger, and isolation. I wanted to gain control of my life, or so I thought. There I was, married with four children and one on the way! I know God's mercy and grace and favor was in my life. Most children who are abused repeat the same abuse. I was with my "bonus" children more than their daddy. Because I was sexually abused, I could have easily repeated that on the children in my care. It was only by the grace of God that I didn't repeat what was done to me; the thought <u>never</u> even came to me. I know God was with me the whole time. My maiden name is Emmanuel, which means "God is with us." I know God was with me. He was right there. I could have gone another way, too. I could have hated the opposite sex because that's who sexually abused me, but God's grace! God put compassion in my heart for all children. I am an advocate for children by the grace of God. I could've turned to drugs and alcohol to self-medicate. My life would have turned out a lot differently if I wasn't covered by grace. I am so grateful that He did not let me out of sight. God entrusted me to raise eight children in all, and He sustained me the whole way. God placed a special love in my heart for children. I truly believe that instead of me repeating the abuse, I have a God-given gift to love all children the way they need to be loved. God's grace was not something I had to buy or something I had to work for. It was all about the love He had for me! It's unconditional love, and the good news is that He loves *you* the same way, too. God's door is always open. It doesn't matter what it is, He is just waiting on you to surrender everything to him just like I did. The hurt, pain, self-blame, isolation, hatred, anger, flashbacks, no self-value, sadness, and hopelessness, I surrendered all of it to Him. He already knew about it anyway.

He was just waiting for me to ask for help, just like He is waiting patiently for you to cry out for help.

He is willing and ready to take the weight you have been carrying. He wants to take the load from you. It's time to surrender. You have been carrying a heavy load far too long. When I look back over my journey, I see that I allowed the abuse to take over my life because I was stuck at nine years old. I allowed it to consume my mind, my thoughts, and my decision-making, and how I looked at the world in general. I wore a mask, and my insides were dead. I kept my physical body in shape and looking good, but my soul and spirit were in terrible shape.

God's grace sustained me until I surrendered, and then He restored me to my rightful position. God's power and grace replaced shame. I have received a double honor.

"Instead of confusion and disgrace, I leap for joy in the presence of my father, for He has given me a double portion." Isaiah 61:6

To restore means to bring back, or return to a previous position. God's grace put me in my right position.

Romans 3:24 says, "I am justified freely by his grace through the redemption that is in Christ."

God is waiting on you to say, "Lord, this is too much for me to handle. I trust you. I give it to you; my life and everything that goes with it." And just watch what happens. God is faithful!

God will guide you in both the good and the difficult times.

No matter what kind of abuse you survived, you can overcome and conquer with the help of God. The effects of sexual abuse WILL NOT GO TO THE NEXT GENERATION. It stops here.

Do you think God's Grace is keeping you right now? If so, how do you know?

Closing Reflections

The first reason I wrote this book is to help someone that has gone through sexual abuse, to let them know that they, too, can overcome and conquer and live a life of fulfillment. The second reason is for my children and grandchildren, so they know what I have been through and to be sure it doesn't happen to anyone else in the family, generation after generation. My prayer is that after reading this book, the readers leave with the knowledge that with God, all things are possible, no matter what.

I gained so much joy and peace writing this book. I felt empowered and liberated and relieved at the same time. I hope and pray that the readers will pass it along to help and encourage someone else. It's my hope that you realize we are only here for a short time, and to take lessons from everything you go through in life so your experiences are not in vain. We are here to help our neighbors. We are here to serve. We are to love and encourage and lift, and sometimes, to carry each other.

I love and enjoy the life God has given me.

(All of my days are good ones, for I have chosen to live the God-kind of life. I have made my unyielding decision to keep my tongue from speaking evil things and to tell the truth in every situation. I have turned from the ways of the wicked and have focused my attention firmly on doing only that which is good. Psalm 34:12-17)

About the Author

Gisele Vann is a down-to-earth person who loves all people, but her heart pulls her to children, whom she loves to be around. Some have said she is a big kid at heart. She has finally discovered her true purpose for being on this earth and in life, and her highest priority is to be an ambassador of the kingdom of God. Knowing this revelation after believing the lies of the enemy for years, she now knows her true identity! She lives her life fearlessly now that she knows the only wise God who walks with her. She exercises the authority she has been given by the Lord. She came from a large family of five boys and four girls. She grew up in Southern California. She was married at age 19 and from that marriage, she became a stepmother to four children. She and her husband went on to have four sons. Two of her sons have dual citizenship, in the U.S. and Italy. Her youngest sons were still at home when her husband lost his battle with colon cancer at the young age of 49. They had been married for 19 ½ years. Gisele did not keep her head down for long. She pushed on and raised four sons. She later met her present husband and has been married to him for seventeen years. She gained a beautiful daughter in this union. She looks at all the children in her life as: *"Gifts from God. They didn't have to come out of my body for them to be my gifts; they all came from God and He blessed me to be their mother."*

Even when you are struggling and fighting to keep your head above the circumstances of life and feeling down about yourself, there is someone admiring and cheering you on in the distance." Gisele "Hicks" Vann

I asked some of my children to describe me when they were children. Here are their responses ...

"Mom was always fearless, unless there was a mouse or a snake involved. Very competitive in any physical outdoor activity or any activity for that matter; always pushed me to not fear, because God has not given us the spirit of fear. She always demanded excellence. When I thought I did my best, she knew I could do better, and I wanted to do better, just for her. I always admired her confidence in just about any situation. I have adopted these traits into my personal life." Jeffrey

"My mom was a constant harbinger for the successful man I would become. Even though I could not fully see that person, she would stress that I could do anything; and I hold that belief today." Jordan

"Growing up, mom was both an enforcer and comforter. When we went through hard times, she never let us kids see her stressed, so we never knew when we were in the midst of a storm. A true woman of God who always shows grit." Emanuel

"To put into words the way I viewed my mom as a child isn't an easy thing to do. This is entirely because I feel like no matter how deep down I dig in an attempt to see how amazing she was to me, I'd still fall short. To me, my mom was love. She loved me unconditionally; the same way she loved all of us. She loved her family and she also loved people. Black people and white people. Old people and young people. Especially children. I watched my mom love on hundreds, and they loved her back. She loved people who didn't love her, and often prayed for them. She never let me down and to me, there was nothing she couldn't do. She was a superhero in my eyes and no one could tell me otherwise." Matthew

"My Mom has always been a strong, fearless fighter who has always put her family first, even in the most challenging circumstances. Her perseverance is inspiring to all who know her story." Joshua

"Auntie Gigi was fun, encouraging and protective. She taught me how to fight back. When I say the wrong thing sometimes, Instead of a harsh word. Auntie Gigi would laugh with surprise and say 'Portia, that's mean' or 'That's not nice, don't say that.' I took her seriously, because I knew she loved me. Auntie Gigi was patient and attentive toward me as a child. The attention felt genuine and safe. As a child I called her 'Mommy Gigi' sometimes, because her tender care for me represented a mothering nature. Auntie Gigi always pushes me to do my best. As I write these words about her, tears are streaming down my face heavily because I'm so grateful that God placed her in my life. My aunt has always encouraged me to live up to my fullest potential in life whether as a child or today as an adult." Portia

"I met Gisele, who is now my mother-in-love nearly 14 years ago. She interviewed me, hired me, and subsequently became my boss. I was in the same position as most of you ... soaking up every ounce of wisdom that she shared as she poured into the lives of young girls unbeknownst to her, into mine as well. I would often get so caught up in her lessons that I would forget that I was actually 'on the clock' until she interrupted my trance with instructions for the day! She is the glue to our family, always rooting for everyone to win and keeping them grounded and connected. Her faith in the Lord is admirable as she never loses sight of who she is and what her assignment is here on earth. I often feel so blessed to have a mother-in-law that I actually LOVE to be around and value her presence in the lives of my own daughters. I am incredibly proud that against all odds she's living out her dreams and putting what I've in action on paper." Dana

"You are allowed to be both a masterpiece and a work in progress at the same time." Author unknown

About the Publishing Support Services:

Motivational M.D. Publishing is a family owned publishing company that assists aspiring authors publish books that heal, uplift, and inspire. It was founded by Dr. Jasmine Zapata who is an award winning author, public health physician, empowerment speaker, mother, and wife. You can connect with Motivational M.D. Publishing team here: www.motivationalmdpublishing.com